MY INK DROPS

DEWDROP IN A DREAM

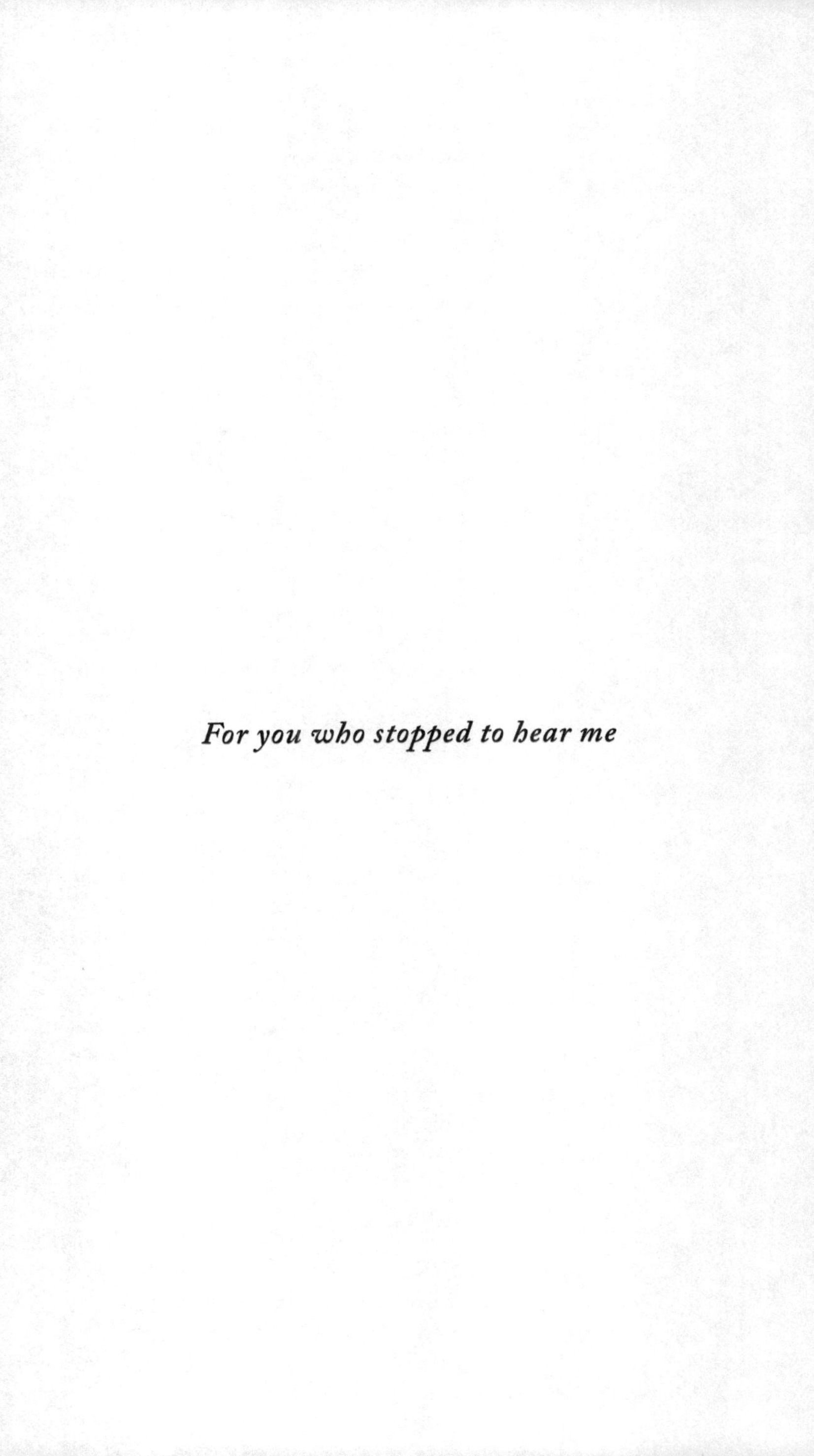

For you who stopped to hear me

Contents

Just the other day I found myself

connecting drops of water

that I spilled on the table

I thought it looked like

a fox pressing a button

Others might perceive it different

They all could have different figures in mind

It could be seen as art but only the I knows about its origin

Art could also be something made

at the spur of the moment

or as a timepass

We just appreciate what we see

without knowing if blood was spilled or water

Only the artist knows the truth behind his art

.

.

.

(Secret of art)

I like you in the depths of

my heart

but on the surface I am following

the crowd

as I am scared to be different

for the fear of not being

accepted

.

.

.

(A Coward)

You make me lift my head
to admire as you stand tall with
elegance
even in this unfamiliar place
no familiar face in sight still you made
it your home

.

.

.

I am not asking you to be honest
from the start just
maintain a little distance
so I know that you aren't
staying forever

.

.

.

(Please)

The more I want to wanna
run away from something or
the more I hate something
the more it gets near me.
It's just like a magnet,
where the poles that
don't match
stick together.

.

.

.

(Magnet of hate)

I wish I could write my life

only depending on my pen.

I don't want to worry about

the quality of the paper,

the colour of the ink, the little

accidents like

spilling water or ink.

.

.

.

(A stupid wish)

When the thought of running away

crosses my mind I try

to forget it.

Cause without being unpredictable,

life maybe seem fair and

content,

but sometimes a happy ending

is not enough.

.

.

.

(I want more)

There have to be no endings
'cause
they are only for the characters,
not the author.
We as characters would be forgotten
when the author
moves to another book.

.

.

.

I want to be an author in the real world,

where I just have to

make a new track whenever

I walk toward doom.

My story will keep on going

not on a smooth highway but on paths

passing through

mountains, valleys, rivers, meadows

with multiple twists and turns;

being imperfect with

perfection.

.

.

.

(Grew up a bit?)

Who are you?

Who are you I wonder as I am judged

Who are you to judge me

Can't I make mistakes

I thought

All I ever saw were prying eyes

And missed the face it belonged to

In the end, it was me

It was my conscience

.

.

.

(It was me)

Why did I turn out like this
Was it society that molded me
Or was it my fault alone
I don't have an answer
Again I wished I had someone
to blame

.

.

.

(A 'me' I don't want)

I know my mistake but

my pride got in between my apology

I thought nothing will change

I thought you will still be there

tomorrow

waiting for me.

But I was wrong

you were gone

.

.

.

(Not wit me anymore)

I am still young, still learning

I know it was my deeds which

lead me here

I regret my choices and

will regret them in the future

as I know I won't change easily

But I still want to say

' I am sorry '

.

.

.

(An apology)

There are times when I forget
who you are,
I start to like you again
and when I remember
the wound that is supposed to heal
just keeps getting deeper

.

.

.

(Forgetting = pain)

My heart beats the loudest in silence

Not because it's terrifying

But the thought that it will be broken

is

.

.

.

(Silence...)

You are like the moon as
you make everything
look beautiful when it comes
under your light

.

.

.

You once asked why don't
I compare you with the sun
The answer is simple,
the sun has the brightest light
but it shows us the things
for how they are,
on the other hand, you make
everything look so dangerously
beautiful

.

.

.

(My moon)

I was so focused on the fact that I was
blamed, I forgot all the times I
was let off the hook
I am ungrateful
Right?

.

.

.

1. There isn't any content, I hope you don't try to find it As this book just contain pieces of me

***

This book has come to
an end, and
I thank you for reading
so far.

***

.

.

.

(Dewdrop in a dream)